IN THE FACE OF TREASON

A Journey Through the Tumultuous Fight for Justice- From Election Controversy to Capitol Siege—Confronting the Forces Seeking to Undermine Democracy

Carter K Miller.

TABLE OF CONTENTS

Introduction

"In the Face of Treason" invites you to embark on a riveting exploration of one such transformative period, from the contentious aftermath of the 2020 presidential election to the shocking siege on the Capitol on January 6th, 2021.

Chapter 1: Foreshadowing a Crisis

The year 2020 stood out as a crucible in American history, a time when the country found itself at a crossroads of its destiny. The stage was set, and the spotlight was firmly fixed on the impending presidential election, but the road leading up to this momentous event was fraught with tension, division, and a slew of challenges that would soon unfold into a crisis of unprecedented proportions.

1.1 The Political Tension Canvas

As the calendar turned to 2020, the United States was on the verge of a political upheaval, with echoes of the past reverberating through the corridors of power, with a nation already deeply divided along ideological lines, and the political climate had become increasingly polarized in the preceding years, setting the stage for a volatile election season. The seeds of discontent were sown in the aftermath of the 2016 election, which was marked by allegations of foreign interference, hacking scandals, and claims of misinformation campaigns. The wounds inflicted by a divisive campaign and unexpected election outcome festered, casting a long shadow over the subsequent years. The rise of populist movements and the amplification of extreme ideologies fueled the flames of discontent, creating an atmosphere ripe for coercion.

The 2020 presidential election loomed large against this backdrop, promising a reckoning for a nation grappling with its identity and the direction of its future. Political discourse had become a battlefield, with social media platforms serving as both the arena and the weapon of choice for political warfare. The polarization that had simmered for years now threatened to boil over, setting the stage for a crisis that would test the resilience of the American democracies.

1.2 Disentangling Controversies

The road to the 2020 election was paved with controversies that sent shockwaves through the political landscape, one of which revolved around the issue of foreign interference, a specter that has haunted the collective consciousness since the 2016 election. Intelligence agencies and experts warned of continued attempts by foreign actors to influence the electoral process, adding an element of uncertainty and distrust to the electoral machinery.

Social media platforms, once hailed as a democratizing force for information, became a breeding ground for disinformation and echo chambers that exacerbated existing divisions. Algorithms designed to maximize user engagement inadvertently facilitated the spread of misinformation, creating a distorted reality for millions of Americans

The debate over election integrity took center stage, with both major political parties raising concerns about the susceptibility of voting systems to tampering. Claims of voter suppression, gerrymandering, and challenges to the legitimacy of mail-in voting added layers of complexity to an already charged environment. Controversies surrounding the postal service's capacity to handle the expected surge in mail-in ballots fueled anxieties about the integrity of the voting system.

Primary elections, once viewed as a democratic ritual, became battlegrounds where factions within parties fought for control and influence.

1.3 Upcoming Challenges

Amid the controversies, a series of challenges emerged, casting a foreboding shadow over the electoral landscape. The specter of a global pandemic, COVID-19, added an unprecedented layer of complexity to the electoral process. The virus, which had already claimed lives and disrupted daily life, prompted a reevaluation of traditional voting methods.

The economic fallout from the pandemic exacerbated the difficulties: unemployment rates skyrocketed, businesses closed, and the very fabric of society appeared to be unraveling. The incumbent administration found itself in uncharted territory, attempting to balance public health concerns with economic imperatives, all while facing a rising tide of public discontent.

In the aftermath of high-profile incidents of police violence and racial injustice, social justice movements gained traction, demanding systemic change; the intersection of these movements with the political landscape added another layer of complexity to an already turbulent year; the demand for societal change clashed with entrenched interests, setting the stage for a battle not only at the ballot box but also in the streets and within the corridors of power.

1.4 The Coming Storm

As political tensions rose, the country found itself at a crossroads, teetering on the brink of a crisis that would reshape its future. The run-up to the 2020 presidential election was marked by a confluence of factors - political polarization, technological challenges, controversies surrounding foreign interference, and a pandemic-induced reckoning.

Chapter 2: The Election Controversy

In the hallowed halls of democracy, the 2020 presidential election in the United States was destined to be etched into the historical tapestry as one of the most contentious and disputed events. As the electoral process unfolded, a cascade of controversies erupted, sparking a firestorm of skepticism and doubt that reverberated across the nation.

2.1 The Problem of Mail-In Voting

With the specter of the COVID-19 pandemic looming large, there was a nationwide push to expand mail-in voting to ensure the safety of voters. However, this move was not without controversy. Claims of potential fraud and concerns about the security of mail-in ballots became a rallying cry for those skeptical of the process.

The sudden shift to widespread mail-in voting, critics argued, created vulnerabilities in the electoral system. Allegations of ballot harvesting, in which individuals or organizations collect and submit ballots on behalf of others, raised concerns about the potential for coercion and fraud. The debate over the authenticity of signatures on mail-in ballots fueled the controversy, with calls for rigorous verification processes to protect the integrity of the electoral system.

Proponents of mail-in voting, on the other hand, argued that it was a necessary response to the challenges posed by the pandemic, emphasizing that instances of fraud were statistically rare and that the benefits of expanded voting access outweighed the risks. The clash between these two perspectives created a divisive narrative that would persist long after the election results were tallied.

2.2 Voter Suppression Claims

As the election progressed, allegations of voter suppression emerged as a recurring theme, particularly in communities with historically marginalized populations. Allegations ranged from restrictive voter ID laws to the closure of polling locations in predominantly minority neighborhoods, and advocacy groups and political activists characterized these measures as deliberate attempts to disenfranchise certain demographics and tip the electoral scales.

The controversy surrounding voter suppression ignited fierce debates about the fundamental principles of democracy. Advocates for stricter voting regulations argued that such measures were necessary to prevent fraud and maintain the integrity of the electoral process. On the other hand, critics contended that these measures disproportionately affected minority communities, echoing a troubling history of systemic disenfranchisement.

Legal battles ensued in various states, with lawsuits challenging the constitutionality of certain voting restrictions. The struggle to balance the need for election security with the imperative to protect the right to vote underscored the deep-rooted divisions within American society.

2.3 The Role of Social Media in Disinformation

In the digital age, the battlefield of information extended far beyond traditional media outlets. Social media platforms became both conduits and amplifiers of information, misinformation, and disinformation. The 2020 election saw a surge in the spread of false narratives, conspiracy theories, and doctored images, creating a volatile environment where discerning fact from fiction became increasingly challenging.

Foreign interference, a specter that haunted the previous election, reared its head once again. Intelligence agencies reported attempts by foreign actors to sow discord, spread misinformation, and undermine confidence in the electoral process. The manipulation of social media platforms by these entities added another layer of complexity to an already fraught situation.

Claims of bias and censorship by social media companies further fueled the controversy. Accusations of selectively suppressing certain political viewpoints or content raised questions about the role and responsibility of these tech giants in shaping public discourse. The intersection of technology, politics, and information became a battleground where the very nature of truth was contested.

2.4 Legal Challenges and Recounts

The aftermath of the election saw a flurry of legal challenges and recount efforts, further intensifying the controversy surrounding the legitimacy of the results. The Trump administration, in particular, mounted a series of legal challenges in key battleground states, alleging irregularities and fraud without presenting concrete evidence. These legal battles unfolded in state and federal courts, reaching the Supreme Court, with each decision contributing to the overall narrative of uncertainty.

Recounts became another focal point of contention. While some argued that recounts were essential to ensure the accuracy of the results, others dismissed them as futile exercises that only served to prolong the inevitable. The recount process itself became a battleground, with accusations of mishandling ballots, partisan interference, and a lack of transparency.

2.5 The Electoral College and Popular Vote Divide

The tension between the electoral college and the popular vote added yet another layer of complexity to the controversy surrounding the 2020 election. As the popular vote favored one candidate, the electoral college painted a different picture. The divide between the two measures of public opinion fueled debates about the efficacy and fairness of the electoral college system.

Calls for electoral reform gained traction, with proponents arguing that the system disproportionately favored certain states and undermined the principle of one person, one vote. The controversy surrounding the electoral college reignited discussions about the need for systemic changes to ensure that the voice of every citizen was equally represented in the highest echelons of government.

2.6 The Polarized Public Sphere

Beyond the specific controversies surrounding the mechanics of the election, the 2020 presidential race laid bare the deep-seated polarization within the American public. The rhetoric employed by political leaders, amplified by media outlets and social media platforms, further entrenched divisions along ideological lines. The erosion of trust in institutions, the media, and even in the electoral process itself created an environment ripe for skepticism and doubt.

Conspiracy theories flourished in this polarized landscape, with factions on both sides of the political spectrum embracing narratives that aligned with their preconceived beliefs. The erosion of a shared reality contributed to an atmosphere where the very notion of objective truth became elusive.

2.7 The Lingering Fallout

As the dust settled on the 2020 election, the controversies that unfolded continued to cast a long shadow over the nation. The fractures exposed during this electoral battle persisted, with mistrust and skepticism becoming enduring features of the political landscape. The aftermath of the election raised profound questions about the resilience of democratic institutions and the fragility of the social contract that underpins the American experiment.

Chapter 3: Democracy Under Siege

On the fateful day of January 6th, 2021, the hallowed halls of the United States Capitol, the symbol of American democracy, became the epicenter of an unprecedented assault. The events that unfolded on that ominous day shook the foundations of the nation and sent shockwaves around the world. This chapter delves into the vivid and chilling account of the siege on the Capitol, capturing the chaos, the violence, and the immediate aftermath that left an indelible mark on the annals of American history.

3.1 The March to Washington

As the sun hung low in the Washington, D.C. sky, a sea of people, united by fervor and political passion, converged on the nation's capital. What began as a rally to protest the certification of the electoral college results swiftly transformed into an ominous spectacle as thousands gathered near the White House, responding to the call of then-President Donald Trump.

The atmosphere was charged with tension and anticipation as the crowd, adorned with flags and banners, made its way towards the Capitol. As they marched, echoes of grievances, fueled by months of political turmoil and contested election results, reverberated through the air. The fervent supporters of Trump, echoing his baseless claims of election fraud, were determined to make their voices heard in the most dramatic and disruptive fashion.

3.2 The Breach of the Capitol

As the crowd approached the Capitol, the mood shifted from passionate protest to something far more sinister. What began as a demonstration turned into an insurrection, and the barricades that stood as a symbolic boundary between the people and their government were breached with an air of brazen defiance.

The breach was a chaotic and surreal spectacle. The Capitol, typically a bastion of order and decorum, was plunged into pandemonium. Rioters, clad in a motley array of attire, surged through the breached barriers, scaling walls, and breaking windows to gain entry. The very heart of American democracy was under siege as the mob descended upon the Capitol Rotunda, Statuary Hall, and the chambers of Congress.

Inside, lawmakers were in the midst of the constitutionally mandated process of certifying the Electoral College results. The joint session of Congress, intended as a ceremonial and routine affair, was abruptly halted as the gravity of the situation became apparent. Evacuation procedures were initiated, and the Capitol, a symbol of stability, order, and the peaceful transition of power, now bore witness to unprecedented chaos.

3.3 The Violent Confrontation

The clash between law enforcement and the insurrectionists intensified as rioters confronted Capitol Police and other security personnel. Tear gas filled the air, and the crackle of flash-bang grenades echoed through the halls. In the chambers of Congress, armed officers barricaded doors, forming a last line of defense against the encroaching mob.

The violence that ensued was captured in shocking images and videos. Rioters rifled through offices, vandalized chambers, and desecrated sacred spaces. The Senate floor, typically a solemn arena of debate, was transformed into a scene of mayhem. The very ideals of democracy were trampled upon as insurrectionists proudly documented their actions, their faces contorted with anger and defiance.

The toll was not only physical but also symbolic. The desecration of the Capitol, the ransacking of offices, and the theft of official items left an indelible scar on the seat of American governance. The echoes of violence reverberated not only through the halls of

Congress but through the collective conscience of the nation.

3.4 The Human Cost

Amidst the chaos, tragedy struck. The day claimed lives, including that of Capitol Police Officer Brian Sicknick, who succumbed to injuries sustained during the clash. Others were injured, both among law enforcement and the rioters. The toll, both in terms of lives lost and the physical injuries inflicted, underscored the gravity of the situation.

The human cost was not limited to the immediate casualties. The trauma endured by those present in the Capitol, the lawmakers, staffers, and journalists who found themselves caught in the maelstrom, resonated long after the physical wounds had healed. The very sanctity of the Capitol, a symbol of the democratic process, was violated in a manner that transcended the physical damage inflicted on the building.

3.5 Immediate Aftereffects

The Capitol, an edifice that had withstood the tests of time and history, bore the scars of an unprecedented assault as the dust settled. The immediate aftermath of the siege saw law enforcement securing the Capitol, clearing out the last remnants of the insurrectionists, and starting the process of restoring order.

The shock and disbelief among lawmakers was palpable; the very institution that had weathered storms, survived wars, and stood tall during moments of national triumph and tragedy had been violated. The resumption of the electoral certification process, which had been delayed by the events, unfolded against a backdrop of shattered windows, hastily erected barricades, and the echoes of the violence that had occurred just hours before.

The response from leaders across the political spectrum was swift and unequivocal: the attack on the Capitol was condemned as an attack on democracy itself. President-elect Joe Biden, in a televised address, condemned the violence and urged the nation to unite. The global community watched in awe and concern as the beacon of democracy flickered but refused to go out.

3.6 The Reckoning and Accountability

The nation faced a reckoning in the aftermath of the Capitol siege, which exposed deep-seated differences that had festered for years, driven by disinformation, political divisiveness, and a contempt for the ideals that support a functional democracy.

The FBI and other law enforcement agencies sifted through a mountain of evidence, including social media posts, videos, and photographs, to build cases against the insurrectionists.

The political fallout was equally seismic, with the role of then-President Donald Trump in inciting the violence being called into question. The House of Representatives quickly moved to impeach the President for a second time, charging him with "incitement of insurrection." The impeachment proceedings, taking place against the backdrop of a nation still reeling from the events of January 6th, added another layer of complexity to an already tumultuous political landscape.

3.7 Democracy's Long-Term Impact

The attack on the Capitol on January 6, 2021, exposed vulnerabilities in the nation's security apparatus and prompted a reevaluation of protocols to safeguard the institutions that underpin the democratic process; the breach became a rallying cry for those advocating for a renewed commitment to the principles of democracy and the rule of law.

The psyche of the country was wounded, and the sense of exceptionalism that often accompanied discussions about American democracy was called into question. The image of the Capitol, adorned with the scars of an insurgency, served as a stark reminder that the foundations of democracy were not impervious to attack.

Chapter 4: Forces at Play-Unmasking the Culprits

The assault on the U.S. Capitol on January 6th, 2021, was a seismic event that sent shockwaves through the foundations of American democracy. Behind the chaos and violence were key individuals and groups who played pivotal roles in orchestrating and participating in the attack. Unmasking the culprits requires a closer examination of the motivations, strategies, and ideologies that fueled this unprecedented breach of the Capitol.

4.1 The Rallying Cry-Trump and His Allies

The events leading up to January 6th were centered on then-President Donald Trump, whose rhetoric and actions played a key role in mobilizing his supporters. In the weeks following the November 2020 election, Trump refused to accept the results, claiming repeatedly without evidence that the election was stolen from him through widespread fraud.

On January 6th, Trump spoke to a crowd of his supporters near the White House, urging them to march to the Capitol and "fight like hell" to overturn the election results. Trump's words served as a rallying cry, providing a veneer of legitimacy to the false claims of election fraud and fueling the anger and frustration that would later boil over into violence.

Several of Trump's allies and staunch supporters also played key roles in promoting the false narrative of a stolen election, including Trump's personal lawyer, Rudy Giuliani, and members of Congress such as Senators Ted Cruz and Josh Hawley, who amplified the unfounded claims, giving the unfounded allegations the appearance of official endorsement.

4.2 Extremist Organizations and Militias

The Proud Boys, a far-right group known for its embrace of political violence, were among those present at the Capitol and actively participated in the breach, engaging in clashes with law enforcement.

The QAnon conspiracy movement, which had gained traction in the preceding years, was also represented among the insurrectionists. QAnon adherents, who believe in a baseless conspiracy involving a secret cabal of Satan-worshipping pedophiles, were part of the mob that descended upon the Capitol. The movement's adherents, often identifiable by QAnon paraphernalia, played a role in spreading disinformation and

The presence of individuals associated with militia groups highlighted the convergence of different extremist factions under a common cause - the rejection of the democratic process. Various militia groups, such as the Oath Keepers and the Three Percenters, were implicated in the planning and execution of the assault. These groups, often characterized by anti-government sentiments, saw the Capitol breach as an opportunity to advance their own agendas.

4.3 Radicalization and Disinformation on the Internet

Social media platforms, particularly Twitter, Facebook, and alternative platforms like Parler, played a critical role in radicalizing individuals and disseminating disinformation that contributed to the Capitol siege.

The spread of disinformation about election fraud, often originating from influential figures and conspiracy theorists, contributed to a distorted perception of reality among those who would later participate in the attack, fueled by echo chambers and algorithmic reinforcement.

The digital space facilitated the rapid dissemination of inflammatory content, creating an environment in which falsehoods could spread unchecked and gain traction among a significant portion of the population. QAnon, in particular, found a home on various online platforms, where adherents exchanged theories, organized events, and amplified their beliefs.

4.4 Influences of White Supremacists and the Far Right

The Capitol siege also revealed the involvement of individuals with ties to white supremacist and far-right ideologies, as evidenced by the presence of Confederate flags, Nazi symbols, and other racist iconography among the insurrectionists.

The Boogaloo Bois, a loosely organized and heavily armed movement, were also present at the Capitol. The Boogaloo Bois, with their distinctive Hawaiian shirts, have been linked to anti-government sentiments and have advocated for armed resistance against perceived tyranny, and their participation in the events of January 6th highlighted the complex web of ideologies that converged to challenge the democratic process.

4.5 Motivations

The motivations behind the Capitol attack were as diverse as the groups involved, with a fervent belief in the false narrative of a stolen election, propagated by Trump and amplified by his allies and online communities, serving as the catalyst for the mobilization of a diverse coalition of groups and individuals.

Some were motivated by anti-government sentiments, seeking to assert their vision of a racially exclusive America, while others were motivated by white supremacist ideologies, seeking to assert their vision of a racially exclusive America. The convergence of these disparate motivations created a volatile mix, with each faction seeing the Capitol siege as an opportunity to advance its own agenda.

4.6 Democratic Undermining Strategies

The Capitol attack was not an isolated act of violence; it was a strategic assault on the democratic process itself, with perpetrators employing a variety of tactics to undermine the electoral system and the institutions that support it.

Disinformation Campaigns: The spread of false narratives about election fraud, as well as the mainstream media's complicity in perpetuating these falsehoods, created a climate of distrust. Disinformation campaigns, often disseminated through social media and fringe platforms, sought to erode public trust in the legitimacy of the electoral process.

Intimidation and Coercion: The storming of the Capitol was an act of physical intimidation, sending a message to lawmakers and the general public alike that the democratic process could be disrupted through force; the breach itself, along with the violence that ensued, was designed to instill fear and convey a threat to the very heart of American governance.

Symbolic Desecration: The use of symbols associated with racism and extremism, such as the Confederate flag and Nazi iconography, was a deliberate choice intended to desecrate the Capitol's symbolic significance; by appropriating these symbols, the attackers sought to communicate a rejection of the Capitol's inclusive and democratic ideals.

Erosion of Trust: Perhaps most insidiously, the attack on the Capitol sought to erode the trust that citizens place in their democratic institutions. By casting doubt on the electoral process, sowing discord, and challenging the peaceful transition of power, the assailants aimed to undermine the very foundation of democracy – the belief that the will of the people is reflected in the outcomes of free and fair elections.

4.7 Legal Consequences and Unanswered Questions

In the aftermath of the Capitol siege, the individuals and groups responsible faced legal consequences. The FBI launched an extensive investigation, leading to arrests and charges against many of those involved. The legal proceedings sought to hold the perpetrators accountable for their roles in the unprecedented attack on the Capitol.

However, the consequences spread beyond the courtroom. The events of January 6th provoked a larger national reassessment, raising issues about the status of American democracy, the role of political leaders in fomenting extremism, and the need for systemic reforms to prevent a repeat.

Key questions remain unanswered, such as how deeply these individuals were radicalized, how much influence disinformation and conspiracy theories had on them, and what role did online echo chambers play in shaping their beliefs and actions. As investigations progressed, the nation grappled with the challenge of comprehending the complex web of factors that contributed to the Capitol attack.

4.8 Healing Wounds and Protecting Democracy

Unmasking the perpetrators of the Capitol siege is a vital step toward comprehending the many factors at work, but it is also critical to address the underlying conditions that allowed these forces to converge in a violent assault on the democratic process.

To heal the damages done on American democracy, a diversified strategy is required:

1. Countering misinformation: Efforts to battle misinformation and restore trust in trustworthy sources of information are critical; media literacy programs, fact-checking campaigns, and ethical online platform policies may all help to reduce the spread of false narratives.

2. Addressing Root Causes: The societal factors that contribute to extremism, such as economic disparities, social inequality, and systemic racism, must be addressed holistically in order to prevent individuals who feel disenfranchised or marginalized from becoming radicalized.

3. Strengthening Cybersecurity: Safeguarding the integrity of the electoral process requires robust cybersecurity measures. Protecting against foreign interference, securing voting systems, and fortifying online platforms against manipulation are critical components of defending democracy in the digital age.

4. Fostering Unity: Fostering a feeling of national unity and common purpose is critical to mending the differences exposed by the Capitol siege, and political leaders, community organizers, and civic institutions all have a role in fostering communication, understanding, and collaboration.

5. Maintaining Accountability: Holding those responsible for the Capitol attack accountable through legal processes sends a clear message that violence and insurgency will not be tolerated, while addressing the root causes of extremism ensures a more comprehensive and long-term resolution.

4.9 The Ongoing Task

The attack on the United States Capitol was a stark reminder that democracy is an ongoing process that requires vigilance and collective effort. Identifying the key individuals and groups responsible for the attack is an important step in understanding the forces at work, but it is only the beginning of a larger journey toward safeguarding the ideals that underpin American democracy.

Chapter 5: Treason's Anatomy

The events of January 6th, 2021, when the United States Capitol was besieged, not only left an indelible mark on the nation's history, but also raised profound legal and constitutional questions. The breach of the Capitol was not a mere act of protest or civil disobedience; it was an unprecedented assault on the democratic process.

5.1 The Legal Environment

The legal landscape surrounding the January 6th events is complex and multifaceted. The actions of those who stormed the Capitol raise a range of legal issues, from trespassing and vandalism to more serious offenses such as assault and sedition. At the heart of these legal considerations is the question of whether the insurrectionists' actions amount to treason under US law.

Trespassing and Vandalism: Many of those involved in the Capitol breach were charged with trespassing and vandalism, which are relatively straightforward charges centered on the physical intrusion into the Capitol building, the destruction of property, and other unlawful activities that occurred during the siege.

Assault and Violence: Individuals who engaged in violent acts against law enforcement officers and others faced assault charges, and the violent clashes that occurred during the breach injured both Capitol Police officers and insurrectionists, prompting a legal response to address the physical harm inflicted.

Sedition: Sedition charges may apply to those who actively participated in the assault on the Capitol with the intent of disrupting the certification of the Electoral College results.

Conspiracy: When individuals combine to do criminal activities, the idea of conspiracy comes into play; some of those engaged in organizing or directing the Capitol siege may face conspiracy charges, reflecting the planned character of the attack.

Weapons and guns Offenses: Possession of weapons and guns on Capitol grounds is absolutely prohibited, and anybody detected carrying or using weapons during the breach may face penalties for unlawful possession and use of firearms.

5.2 American Legal Treason

The concept of treason is deeply rooted in American history, as reflected in Article III, Section 3, which defines treason as "levying war against [the United States], or in adhering to their enemies, giving them aid and comfort." However, the Constitution provides a narrow and specific definition of treason to guard against its misuse as a tool for political persecution.

Two witnesses must testify to the same overt act or the accused must confess in open court for an act to qualify as treason under the Constitution. This stringent requirement reflects the framers' desire to prevent the broad and arbitrary use of treason charges, ensuring that only the most serious and provable offenses fall under this category.

Treason includes the following elements:

1. Levying War: The act must entail the use of force or violence, resulting in a war against the United States, distinguishing treason from other offenses and emphasizing the seriousness of the conduct.

2. Adhering to Enemies: Treason also includes offering assistance and comfort to enemies of the United States, emphasizing the nation's betrayal and participation with those pursuing its demise.

5.3 Treason's Importance in the Capitol Siege

While the legal charges brought against those involved in the Capitol siege may include sedition, conspiracy, and weapons-related offenses, the specific charge of treason may be more difficult to apply, due to the narrow definition and stringent evidentiary requirements outlined in the Constitution.

Levying War: Whether the insurrectionists' actions amounted to "levying war" against the United States is a complicated legal issue. Traditionally, levying war has been interpreted to involve a state of open armed conflict against the government. The Capitol siege, while violent, may not fit the traditional understanding of a war in the conventional sense.

Adhering to Enemies: The concept of adhering to enemies requires a demonstration of allegiance to a foreign entity or group actively engaged in hostilities against the United States. In the context of the Capitol siege, the primary actors were domestic extremists rather than agents of a foreign power. While the attack may have indirectly benefited foreign adversaries by sowing discord, proving direct adherence to foreign enemies could be challenging.

5.4 Political Ramifications and Accountability

While the legal concept of treason may create obstacles in applying it directly to the Capitol siege, the events of January 6th highlighted serious political and ethical considerations about responsibility and the preservation of democratic principles.

The Betrayal of Trust: The Capitol breach represented a betrayal of the trust bestowed by the American people on elected leaders and institutions; the attack was not only an assault on the physical structure of democracy, but also an affront to the intangible ideals that bind the nation together.

Consequences for Political Leaders: The actions of political leaders who played a role in inciting or endorsing the events of January 6th raised questions about accountability. While legal charges against elected officials exercising their constitutional rights to free speech may be difficult to apply, the ethical implications of their rhetoric and actions remain a matter of public scrutiny.

National Reckoning: The Capitol siege prompted a national reckoning about the state of American democracy, the role of political leaders in shaping public discourse, and the need for reforms to safeguard the institutions that underpin the democratic process, which went beyond legal ramifications to include broader questions about the nation's democratic foundations.

5.5 Lessons Learned and Next Steps

The events of January 6, 2021 serve as a sobering reminder of the fragility of democratic institutions and the importance of protecting them from internal threats. As the country grapples with the legal, political, and ethical dimensions of the Capitol siege, there are valuable lessons to be learned and a path forward to strengthen democracy.

1. Increasing Legal Safeguards: The legal response to the Capitol siege highlighted the need for a robust and adaptable legal framework to address threats to the democratic process. Legislative efforts to strengthen laws against domestic extremism, sedition, and other offenses that undermine democracy can contribute to a more resilient legal system.

2. Reinforcing Constitutional Principles: Because the Constitution serves as the foundation for the American system of governance, it is critical to ensure a shared understanding of constitutional principles and their application in times of crisis in order to uphold the rule of law and the integrity of democratic institutions.

3. Fostering Civic Education: Promoting civic education is crucial for cultivating an informed and engaged citizenry. A populace equipped with a deep understanding of democratic principles, the rule of law, and the responsibilities of citizenship is better equipped to recognize and resist attempts to subvert the democratic process.

4. Addressing Extremism's Root Causes: The Capitol siege drew attention to the underlying factors that contribute to extremism, such as economic inequality, social injustice, and political polarization; addressing these root causes will necessitate comprehensive efforts to build a more inclusive and equitable society.

5. Rebuilding Trust: Restoring trust in democratic institutions is a collaborative effort, with political leaders, community organizers, and citizens all contributing to a climate of transparency, accountability, and open dialogue.

While legal charges may capture specific offenses committed by those who breached the Capitol, the larger challenge is addressing the erosion of democratic norms and principles that allowed such an attack to occur.

The events of January 6th, 2021 serve as a stark reminder of the ongoing struggle to preserve the ideals of democracy and ensure that the nation remains resilient in the face of internal conflict.

Chapter 6: A Nation's Reaction- Outrage and Unification

The Capitol siege on January 6, 2021, was a moment of profound shock and disbelief that reverberated not only through the halls of American democracy, but across the entire nation and the world. In this chapter, we examine the multifaceted response to the unprecedented attack on the United States Capitol, examining the outrage that ensued as well as the moments of unity and resilience that emerged in the face of a threat to democracy.

6.1 The Immediate Reaction

The scenes of violence and chaos at the Capitol elicited a swift and widespread outcry from across the political spectrum. Political leaders, both Democrats and Republicans, condemned the attack on the heart of American democracy in unequivocal terms. President-elect Joe Biden, who will take office just weeks later, addressed the nation with a message of unity and denounced the violence as an attack on the nation's very fabric.

International leaders, too, expressed shock and concern about the events unfolding in the United States, with allies and adversaries alike weighing in on the global ramifications of an attack on the symbol of democracy. The Capitol siege served as a stark reminder that democratic principles are not immune to challenge, even within the borders of one of the world's oldest democracies.

6.2 Unity in the Face of Chaos

While the Capitol siege exposed deep divisions in American society, it also sparked moments of unity and resilience. Among the chaos, stories of bravery emerged: Capitol Police officers risking their lives to protect lawmakers, elected officials reaching across party lines in the face of a common threat, and citizens banding together to condemn the violence and defend democratic values.

Bipartisan Condemnation: The attack on the Capitol prompted an unprecedented joint session of Congress to resume the certification of the Electoral College results later that same evening. Despite the traumatic events that had unfolded just hours earlier, lawmakers reconvened to fulfill their constitutional duty. The resumption of the proceedings, marked by bipartisan condemnation of the violence, sent a powerful message of unity and resilience.

Law Enforcement Resilience: The resilience of law enforcement officers who faced the brunt of the violence became a symbol of strength and commitment to upholding the rule of law, as many officers displayed extraordinary courage in defending the Capitol and those inside, despite being outnumbered and facing a hostile mob.

Community Response: Across the nation, communities expressed their outrage and solidarity in various ways. Vigils, marches, and gatherings took place to denounce the attack on democracy and call for unity. The response extended beyond political affiliations, with citizens from diverse backgrounds coming together to reaffirm their commitment to democratic principles.

6.3 Repercussions on the Global Stage

Internationally, the Capitol siege prompted a reassessment of the United States' standing as a bastion of democracy. Allies who had long looked to the U.S. as a model of stable governance expressed concern about the erosion of democratic norms. Adversaries seized the opportunity to criticize the perceived weaknesses of American democracy, framing the events as evidence of internal strife and institutional vulnerability.

The global response underscored the interconnected nature of democracy and the impact of events within one nation on the perceptions of democratic governance worldwide. The attack on the Capitol prompted introspection not only within the United

States but also among nations grappling with their own democratic challenges.

6.4 Condemnation and Reflection

In the aftermath of the Capitol siege, the nation engaged in a process of collective condemnation and reflection. The events served as a catalyst for introspection on the state of American democracy, the role of political leaders in shaping public discourse, and the need for reforms to safeguard the institutions that underpin the democratic process.

Political Fallout: The attack on the Capitol had immediate political consequences. Calls for accountability reverberated across the political spectrum, leading to investigations, resignations, and calls for the impeachment of then-President Donald Trump. The House of Representatives moved swiftly to impeach Trump for a second time, charging him with "incitement of insurrection."

Corporate Response: Corporations and business leaders also responded to the events with a mixture of condemnation and concrete actions. Social media platforms, in particular, took steps to address the spread of misinformation and hate speech. The suspension of then-President Trump's accounts on major social media platforms marked a significant moment in the relationship between technology companies and political discourse.

Media Scrutiny: The role of the media in shaping public perception and discourse came under increased scrutiny. Questions were raised about the responsibility of media outlets in disseminating information and the potential impact of sensationalism and partisan coverage on public sentiment. The events of January 6th prompted a renewed conversation about the role of journalism in fostering an informed and engaged citizenry.

6.5 The Role of Social Media

The Capitol siege brought to the forefront the role of social media platforms in shaping public discourse and facilitating the spread of misinformation. The planning and coordination of the attack, along with the dissemination of false narratives about election fraud, were facilitated through online channels. The events prompted a reevaluation of the role and responsibility of social media companies in moderating content and preventing the use of their platforms for the incitement of violence.

Content Moderation: The suspension of then-President Trump's accounts on major social media platforms, including Twitter and Facebook, raised questions about the power of private companies in moderating public discourse. The actions of these platforms, while applauded by some for curbing the spread of disinformation, also ignited debates about the limits of corporate control over public speech.

Misinformation and Extremism: The Capitol siege highlighted the need to address the spread of misinformation and the role of online platforms in amplifying extremist ideologies. Efforts to combat online radicalization, enhance content moderation, and promote media literacy gained renewed attention as part of a broader strategy to mitigate the influence of disinformation.

6.6 The Resilience of Democracy

While the Capitol siege laid bare vulnerabilities within the democratic system, it also showcased the resilience of democratic institutions and the commitment of individuals to upholding democratic values. The resumption of the electoral certification process on the same day as the attack demonstrated a commitment to the rule of law and the continuity of democratic governance.

Inauguration Day: The peaceful transfer of power on Inauguration Day, January 20th, 2021, marked a symbolic triumph of democracy over the forces that sought to undermine it. The inauguration of President Joe Biden and Vice President Kamala

Harris served as a testament to the endurance of democratic norms and the capacity of the nation to overcome internal challenges.

National Guard Deployment: The deployment of National Guard troops to secure the Capitol in the wake of the attack showcased the capacity of the United States to respond to threats to its democratic institutions. The visible presence of the National Guard during the inauguration reinforced the commitment to protecting the peaceful transition of power.

Global Solidarity: The global response to the Capitol siege also included expressions of solidarity with the American people and their commitment to democratic principles. Leaders from around the world, representing diverse political systems, offered messages of support and emphasized the importance of safeguarding democratic norms.

6.7 Lessons Learned and Moving Forward

The response to the Capitol siege, characterized by outrage, unity, and resilience, yielded valuable lessons for the United States and the broader international community.

1. Protecting Democratic Norms: The events of January 6th highlighted the importance of actively safeguarding democratic norms and institutions; the attack prompted a reevaluation of security protocols, the role of the media, and the role of the government in law enforcement, as well as the need for vigilant protection of the democratic process.

2. Addressing Systemic Issues: The Capitol siege brought to light systemic issues in American society, such as political polarization, economic inequality, and racial injustice, which must be addressed in order to build a more inclusive and resilient democracy.

3. Global Interconnectedness: The global response to the Capitol siege highlighted the interconnected nature of democracies worldwide. The events prompted a renewed commitment to defending democratic principles and fostering international cooperation to address common challenges.

4. Strengthening Civic Education: Enhancing civic education emerged as a crucial component of fortifying democracy. Promoting a deep understanding of democratic principles, the rule of law, and the responsibilities of citizenship is essential for fostering an informed and engaged citizenry.

5. Technology and Democracy: The role of technology, particularly social media, in shaping public discourse and facilitating the spread of misinformation became a focal point for reform.

Addressing the challenges posed by online radicalization and disinformation requires a comprehensive and collaborative approach involving governments, technology companies, and civil society.

6.8 The Ongoing Challenge
The events of January 6th, 2021, represented a watershed moment in the history of American democracy. The response to the Capitol siege, characterized by outrage and unity, laid bare the challenges and opportunities for safeguarding democratic values in an era of complex threats.

Chapter 7: Justice on Trial

The aftermath of the Capitol siege on January 6th, 2021, was marked by a swift and determined effort to hold those responsible accountable for their actions. This chapter chronicles the legal proceedings and investigations that unfolded in the wake of the attack on the U.S. Capitol, delving into the complexities and challenges of seeking justice for an unprecedented assault on American democracy.

7.1 The Legal Response Unveiled

In the immediate aftermath of the Capitol siege, law enforcement agencies, including the Federal Bureau of Investigation (FBI), launched a massive and unprecedented effort to identify, apprehend, and prosecute those involved in the attack. The legal response was multifaceted, encompassing a range of charges from trespassing to sedition, reflecting the gravity of the events that transpired on that fateful day.

Arrests and Charges: The weeks following the Capitol breach saw a wave of arrests as law enforcement agencies, aided by tips from the public and evidence collected from social media, identified individuals involved in the attack. Charges ranged from relatively minor offenses such as trespassing and disorderly conduct to more serious charges including assault, conspiracy, and sedition.

Sedition Charges: The application of sedition charges, a rare and severe offense, signaled the gravity with which law enforcement viewed the attack on the Capitol. Sedition involves attempting to overthrow the government or prevent the execution of federal law through force. Those charged with sedition were accused of actively participating in the violence with the intent of disrupting the certification of the Electoral College results.

Investigations into Conspiracy: The concept of conspiracy emerged prominently in legal proceedings, with investigators examining the coordinated planning and organization that preceded the attack. The identification of individuals and groups involved in conspiracy to commit violence against the government became a focal point of the investigations.

7.2 Legal Challenges and Complexities

The legal response to the Capitol siege was met with a host of challenges and complexities, reflecting the unprecedented nature of the attack and the diverse motivations of those involved.

Identification and Differentiation: One of the primary challenges faced by investigators was the identification and differentiation of individuals within the large and diverse mob that stormed the Capitol. The sheer scale of the attack, combined with the use of masks and other tactics to conceal identities, complicated efforts to attribute specific actions to particular individuals.

Constitutional Protections: The legal proceedings were conducted within the framework of constitutional protections afforded to all individuals, even those accused of participating in the attack. Legal experts grappled with questions of free speech, assembly, and the delicate balance between ensuring justice and respecting constitutional rights.

Online Radicalization: The role of online platforms in radicalizing individuals and coordinating the attack posed a unique challenge for law enforcement. Investigations delved into the digital footprint of suspects, examining social media posts, online forums, and encrypted messaging platforms to establish patterns of coordination and planning.

International Ramifications: The global nature of the attack, with its reverberations felt around the world, introduced international legal considerations. The involvement of individuals from various countries raised questions about the extradition and prosecution of those residing outside the United States.

7.3 Landmark Cases and Legal Precedents

As court processes proceeded, several instances emerged as milestones, offering insight on the complexity and precedents created by the Capitol siege investigations.

The Oath Keepers and Proud Boys: The involvement of organized groups such as the Oath Keepers and Proud Boys drew particular attention. Members of these groups faced charges ranging from conspiracy to obstruction of an official proceeding. The legal scrutiny of organized extremist groups highlighted the potential for such entities to pose a direct threat to the democratic process.

Individual Accountability: Legal proceedings also focused on individuals who played prominent roles in the attack, including those who breached the Capitol building, assaulted law enforcement officers, and engaged in acts of vandalism. The question of individual accountability underscored the principle that each participant, regardless of affiliation or motivation, must face the legal consequences of their actions.

Digital Forensics and Evidence: The reliance on digital forensics and evidence collected from online platforms became a hallmark of the investigations. The analysis of social media posts, geolocation data, and communications provided crucial insights into the planning and execution of the attack.

7.4 The Role of Political Leaders

The judicial reaction to the Capitol siege prompted concerns about the possible culpability of political leaders who helped shape the narrative that spurred the attack.

Impeachment Proceedings: In the political realm, the House of Representatives moved forward with impeachment proceedings against then-President Donald Trump for a second time. The articles of impeachment charged Trump with "incitement of insurrection" based on his rhetoric before and during the Capitol siege. The Senate trial that followed addressed the question of whether a sitting president could be held accountable for actions perceived as incitement to violence.

Public Officials Under Investigation: Beyond the presidency, the legal response examined the role of other public officials who endorsed and amplified false claims about the election. While the legal system distinguishes between protected political speech and actions that incite violence, the Capitol siege prompted a broader discussion about political leaders' responsibility in shaping public discourse.

7.5 The Pursuit of Accountability

Accountability for the events of January 6th stretched beyond judicial processes to include a greater national reckoning.

Truth and Reconciliation: A bipartisan commission to investigate the Capitol siege, modeled after the 9/11 Commission, was proposed as a mechanism for uncovering the truth and promoting national reconciliation. The proposed commission, modeled after the 9/11 Commission, aimed to conduct a comprehensive and non-partisan investigation into the factors leading to the attack and the response of law enforcement.

Healing and Rebuilding faith: The legal reaction was entwined with larger attempts to heal the wounds inflicted on American democracy; restoring faith in democratic institutions necessitated openness, accountability, and a commitment to tackling the core causes of the attack.

National Reflection: The legal proceedings prompted a national reflection on the fragility of democracy and the collective responsibility to protect its institutions, with civic organizations, educational institutions, and community leaders collaborating to promote dialogue, understanding, and a shared commitment to democratic values.

7.6 The Ongoing Task

The legal response to the Capitol siege was a watershed moment in American history, addressing the immediate aftermath of an unprecedented attack on the United States Capitol; however, the pursuit of justice and accountability remains a constant challenge, one that extends beyond individual prosecutions to broader questions about the state of American democracy.

The events of January 6th, 2021 serve as a stark reminder of the ongoing struggle to preserve the ideals of democracy and ensure that the nation remains resilient in the face of internal conflict.

Chapter 8: The Difficult Battle for Democracy

The aftermath of the Capitol siege on January 6th, 2021, marked a watershed moment in American history, sparking a tumultuous battle for the restoration and fortification of democratic processes. This chapter traces the efforts made by individuals and institutions to restore faith in democracy, examining legislative and societal responses aimed at fortifying the nation's democratic ideals.

8.1 Restoring Democracy's Trust

The attack on the United States Capitol exposed the flaws in American democracy, calling into question the very essence of the country's founding principles. In the aftermath of the unprecedented events of January 6th, a collective determination emerged to restore faith in democratic processes and strengthen the resilience of the country's democratic institutions.

Transparency and Accountability: A commitment to transparency and accountability was one of the key pillars in restoring faith in democracy. Efforts were made to ensure a thorough and impartial investigation into the events of January 6th, with a focus on uncovering the truth and holding those responsible accountable. The proposed establishment of a bipartisan commission aimed to provide a comprehensive examination of the factors leading to the attack and the responsibility of those responsible.

Rebuilding Trust in Institutions: The attack on the Capitol had eroded trust in democratic institutions, including the electoral process and government functioning; steps were taken to rebuild this trust through clear communication, adherence to democratic norms, and a commitment to upholding the rule of law. Political leaders, both elected and appointed, played an important role in conveying a sense of stability and commitment to democratic values.

Civic Engagement and Education: Recognizing the importance of an informed and engaged citizenry, efforts were made to promote civic education and awareness. Civic organizations, educational institutions, and community leaders took on the task of fostering a deeper understanding of democratic principles, the rule of law, and the responsibilities of citizenship.

8.2 Legislative Solutions to Strengthen Democracy

Following the Capitol siege, legislative measures were offered to address structural concerns, strengthen democratic processes, and protect the nation from future attacks.

Election Integrity Measures: The attack on the Capitol was fueled in part by false claims of election fraud. To address these concerns, lawmakers introduced measures aimed at strengthening the electoral process, such as enhanced security protocols, audits, and measures to combat disinformation.

Domestic Extremism Legislation: The involvement of organized extremist groups in the Capitol siege prompted a reevaluation of domestic extremism laws, with legislative efforts aimed at equipping law enforcement with the tools necessary to combat the threat posed by individuals and groups seeking to undermine the democratic process through violence.

Campaign Finance Reform: In the aftermath of the attack, the role of money in politics was called into question, and legislative proposals aimed at campaign finance reform sought to limit the influence of money in shaping political discourse and ensure a more equitable and transparent electoral system.

Security and readiness: The Capitol hack highlighted flaws in security and readiness, prompting legislative action to beef up security measures at the Capitol and other critical government institutions, assuring a more robust reaction to possible attacks.

8.3 Societal Reactions and Popular Movements

Beyond legislative measures, social responses and grassroots movements were critical in the fight for democracy, with ordinary individuals, activists, and organizations all contributing to the continuous effort to strengthen democratic principles.

Pro-Democracy Movements: In the aftermath of the Capitol siege, grassroots organizations, advocacy groups, and activists mobilized to defend democratic principles, promote inclusivity, and counter extremist ideologies, with the goal of creating a groundswell of support for the foundations of democracy.

Community Dialogues: To foster understanding and unity within communities, community leaders organized town halls, discussions, and forums to facilitate conversations about the state of democracy, the importance of civic participation, and strategies for building resilient communities.

Media Literacy Campaigns: Recognizing the role of the media in shaping public perception, media literacy campaigns were launched to provide citizens with the skills needed to distinguish reliable information from misinformation, with the goal of improving critical thinking and encouraging responsible consumption of news and information.

Youth Engagement: In the fight for democracy, young people in particular emerged as a driving force, with youth-led movements, activism, and civic engagement initiatives seeking to amplify the voices of the next generation and cultivate a sense of responsibility for the future of democratic governance.

8.4 Global Views and Collaboration

The events of January 6th, 2021, had worldwide consequences, forcing a global assessment on the condition of democracy and the linked nature of democratic government; the battle for democracy expanded beyond national borders, with international collaboration playing an important role.

International Solidarity: In the aftermath of the Capitol siege, leaders and citizens from around the world expressed solidarity with the American people, emphasizing the shared commitment to democratic values and the recognition of democracy as a collective endeavor that transcends national boundaries.

Democracy Promotion Initiatives: The attack on the United States Capitol triggered a renewed focus on democracy promotion initiatives, with nations and organizations throughout the world working to support democratic government, safeguard human rights, and strengthen the resilience of democratic institutions.

Diplomacy and Alliances: The events of January 6th highlighted the importance of diplomatic efforts and alliances in preserving democratic values, with international partnerships used to address common challenges such as the rise of extremism, disinformation campaigns, and threats to democratic norms.

8.5 Criticisms and Challenges

Despite concerted attempts to strengthen democracy, the fight met hurdles and criticism, including the following:

Political Polarization: Deep-seated political polarization within the United States posed a significant barrier to unity and collaboration, making efforts to strengthen democracy difficult to achieve consensus on legislative measures and societal responses.

Misinformation and Disinformation: The pervasive spread of misinformation and disinformation hampered efforts to restore trust in democratic processes, and addressing the root causes of false narratives and conspiracy theories proved to be a complex challenge requiring a multifaceted approach.

Threats to Democratic Norms: The fight for democracy extended beyond the immediate aftermath of the Capitol siege to confront systemic issues that threatened the foundations of democratic governance.

8.6 Lessons Learned and Next Steps

The stormy battle for democracy that followed the Capitol siege offered important lessons and insights for the nation and the global world.

1. Democratic Values' Resilience: The events of January 6th highlighted the resilience of democratic values and the capacity of individuals and institutions to respond to threats, and the fight for democracy became a testament to the enduring commitment to the principles that underpin democratic governance.

2. Importance of Civic Engagement: Civic engagement emerged as a linchpin in fortifying democracy, with citizens' active participation in the democratic process, from voting to community dialogue, proving critical in shaping the nation's trajectory and countering threats to democratic norms.

3. Global Interconnectedness: The global response to the Capitol siege highlighted the global interconnectedness of democracies, with international coordination and solidarity acknowledged as critical components in protecting democratic ideals and tackling common concerns.

4. Addressing the Root Causes: Attempts to Fortifying democracy went beyond addressing immediate symptoms to addressing the root causes of societal divisions, political polarization, and the spread of extremism; a comprehensive approach was required to create a more resilient democratic system.

5. Continual Vigilance: The fight for democracy was framed as an ongoing, dynamic process that necessitated constant vigilance and adaptation on the part of the nation and its allies in the face of evolving threats to democratic governance.

Chapter 9: Learning Experiences

The turbulent journey that followed the events of 2020 and 2021 prompted a deep and introspective examination of the American democratic system, and this chapter reflects on the lessons learned, evaluating the vulnerabilities exposed, and considering the implications for democracy's future.

9.1 Democracy's Unraveling Tapestry
As the nation grappled with the aftermath of the Capitol siege, lessons emerged that demanded attention, reflection, and, most importantly, a commitment to fortifying the democratic foundations.

1. Resilience in the Face of Vulnerabilities: The resilience of democracy was demonstrated by institutions' ability to withstand unprecedented challenges; the fact that the electoral process continued despite attempts to disrupt it demonstrated the durability of democratic norms; however, the events exposed vulnerabilities that required careful consideration and strategic fortification.

2. Civic Education's Importance: Civic education has emerged as a cornerstone in the development of a robust and informed citizenry, with the dissemination of accurate information, understanding of democratic principles, and critical thinking skills becoming critical components in immunizing the public against the corrosive effects of misinformation and disinformation.

3. Fragility of Trust: While the attack on the Capitol eroded trust in democratic institutions, subsequent efforts to restore faith demonstrated that trust could be rebuilt through transparency, accountability, and a renewed commitment to democratic values.

4. Role of Political Leadership: The events highlighted the influential role of political leaders in shaping public discourse and perceptions, with far-reaching consequences. The responsibility of political leaders in upholding democratic norms and fostering national unity became a critical lesson.

9.2 Democratic System Vulnerabilities

The arduous voyage showed vulnerabilities within the democratic system, focusing light on areas that required adjustment to preserve the ongoing strength of American democracy.

1. Political Polarization: Perhaps the most glaring vulnerability was the deep-seated political polarization that permeated the nation. The widening ideological divide fueled mistrust, hindered collaboration, and created an environment where compromise became increasingly challenging. Addressing this polarization was fundamental to fortifying the democratic system.

2. Threats to Election Integrity: The events surrounding the 2020 presidential election brought to the forefront the vulnerability of the electoral process. False claims of widespread voter fraud and attempts to undermine the legitimacy of the election posed a direct threat to the core democratic principle of free and fair elections. Safeguarding election integrity became a paramount concern.

3. Impact of Disinformation: The power of disinformation and misinformation to manipulate public opinion and incite violence was starkly evident. The events leading up to the Capitol siege highlighted the need for robust strategies to combat the spread of false narratives, particularly in the digital age where information can be disseminated rapidly and widely.

The ease with which a mob breached the symbol of American democracy raised questions about the adequacy of security measures and the readiness of institutions to respond to threats, making strengthening security protocols and preparedness imperative.

9.3 Democratic Strengthening Pathways

The lessons learned from the turbulent journey provided an opportunity for the country to embark on paths that would strengthen its democratic foundations. Addressing vulnerabilities required a multifaceted approach that included legislative reforms, civic engagement initiatives, and a commitment to fostering a more inclusive and resilient democracy.

1. Legislative Reforms: Legislative reforms aimed at enhancing election integrity, such as robust auditing processes, increased transparency in vote counting, and measures to address concerns about voter suppression, were critical in fortifying the democratic process. The goal was to boost public confidence in the electoral system.

2. Institutional Strengthening: The events emphasized the importance of fortifying democratic institutions against external threats, which included investing in law enforcement training and capacity, improving cybersecurity measures, and ensuring that institutions responsible for upholding democratic values were prepared to face challenges.

3. Civic Education Initiatives: Recognizing the importance of civic education in developing informed citizens, initiatives were launched to improve civics curriculum in schools and promote ongoing civic education for adults, with the goal of providing individuals with the knowledge and skills necessary to actively participate in the democratic process.

4. Combating Disinformation: Collaborative efforts involving government agencies, technology companies, and civil society gained prominence in order to identify and counter false narratives, limit the spread of misinformation, and foster a media landscape that prioritized accuracy and accountability.

5. National Reconciliation Efforts: Restoring trust required concerted efforts toward national reconciliation, with initiatives aimed at bringing together communities divided along political lines, fostering dialogue, and finding common ground, with the goal of healing the wounds inflicted on the social fabric and rebuilding a sense of national unity.

9.4 International Cooperation

Lessons learned transcended national boundaries, emphasizing the importance of international cooperation in preserving and promoting democratic values.

1. International Alliances and Partnerships in Defending Democracy: The global response to the events of 2020 and 2021 highlighted the interconnectedness of democratic nations, and international alliances and partnerships became instrumental in defending democracy, countering authoritarian influences, and promoting the principles of freedom and self-governance.

2. Learning from Global Experiences: As nations around the world faced their own democratic challenges, the exchange of experiences and best practices became valuable, providing insights into effective strategies for protecting democratic institutions and countering threats.

3. Diplomacy for Democratic Governance: Nations engaged in diplomatic efforts to support democratic movements, advocate for human rights, and foster international cooperation in addressing common challenges to democracy.

9.5 The Ongoing Adventure

The nation was at a crossroads, with the opportunity to leverage the insights gained and chart a course toward a more resilient and inclusive democratic future.

1. Continuous Adaptation: Because threats to democracy evolve, the nation must remain vigilant, agile, and responsive to emerging challenges, recognizing that defending democracy is an ongoing and dynamic process.

2. Engaging the Next Generation: The commitment to democracy extended to future generations, with efforts to engage and educate young people in democratic governance principles essential for laying the groundwork for active and informed citizenship that would last for years.

3. Fostering a Culture of Respect: The lessons learned emphasized the importance of cultivating a culture of respect and understanding, with political leaders, institutions, and citizens all needing to prioritize respectful discourse, empathy, and collaboration in order to bridge divides.

4. Embracing variety: A healthy democracy thrives on variety. Diverse viewpoints, experiences, and backgrounds were essential in establishing an inclusive democratic society that mirrored the diversity of its citizens.

9.6 The Journey Ahead

The road ahead was difficult, but the lessons learned provided a compass for navigating the complexities of the democratic journey; the nation faced the task of translating these lessons into tangible actions, forging a path toward a future in which democracy stood resilient, inclusive, and steadfast against the forces that sought to undermine it.

As the country reflected on its turbulent journey, Abraham Lincoln's words rang true: "A house divided against itself cannot stand." The lessons learned served as a reminder that democracy's strength lay in unity, resilience, and a shared commitment to the principles that had guided the country throughout its history.

Conclusion

From the controversies surrounding the 2020 election to the unprecedented Capitol siege on January 6th, 2021, "In the Face of Treason: A Journey Through the Tumultuous Fight for Justice" is more than just a chronicle of events; it is a testament to the resilience of democracy and the enduring commitment of a nation to confront challenges head-on.

The tumultuous fight for justice, democracy, and the rule of law has been a collective journey—one that has demanded introspection, resilience, and recommitment to the values that define the nation.

The narrative then plunged into the heart of the storm, vividly painting the events of January 6th, 2021, when the Capitol was besieged—a day that will forever be etched in the annals of American history. The book began with a prelude to a crisis, examining the political tensions that set the stage for the tumultuous events that followed. It unfolded with an exploration of election controversies, delving into the claims and counterclaims that ignited

The voyage continued with a look at the efforts taken by individuals and organizations to restore trust in democratic processes, including legislative measures, social movements, and grassroots activities aimed at bolstering democracy's foundations.

The resilient spirit of democracy shines through as the book concludes, and the United States has an opportunity to reaffirm its role as a global beacon of democracy, leading by example and collaborating with like-minded nations. The challenges faced are significant, but the lessons learned and proposed measures provide a roadmap for navigating the complexities of the democratic journey.

"In the Face of Treason" is a call to action, challenging each citizen to play an active role in shaping the nation's democratic future. The pages may close, but the journey continues—an ongoing commitment to the ideals that form the bedrock of a free and just society.

As the story concludes, it leaves behind a narrative that is not just a reflection of the past but a guide for the future—a future shaped by an unwavering commitment to democratic values.